COLLEGE OF ALAMEDA LIBRARY

D0338395

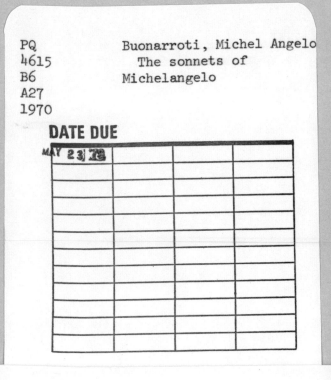

PQ
4615
B6
A27
1970

Buonarroti, Michel Angelo
    The sonnets of
Michelangelo

DATE DUE

MAY 23 78			

LENDING POLICY

IF YOU DAMAGE OR LOSE LIBRARY
MATERIALS, THEN YOU WILL BE
CHARGED FOR REPLACEMENT. FAIL-
URE TO PAY AFFECTS LIBRARY
PRIVILEGES, GRADES, TRANSCRIPTS,
DIPLOMAS, AND REGISTRATION
PRIVILEGES OR ANY COMBINATION
THEREOF.

THE SONNETS
OF
MICHELANGELO

THE
SONNETS
OF
MICHELANGELO

Translated by Elizabeth Jennings
With a selection of Michelangelo drawings
and an introduction by Michael Ayrton

WITHDRAWN

1970

DOUBLEDAY & COMPANY, INC., GARDEN CITY, NEW YORK

Library of Congress Catalog Card Number 71–89122
Copyright © 1961 by The Folio Society Limited
All Rights Reserved
Printed in the United States of America
First Edition in the United States of America

CONTENTS

ILLUSTRATIONS

[7]

12. Wrestlers. Red chalk, about 1513. Louvre. *Cabinet des Dessins, Musee du Louvre.*

13. Study for the Cascina Cartoon. Black chalk, about 1520. *Teyler Museum, Haarlem.*
14. Christ on the Cross. Black chalk, 1540–1541. *British Museum. Trustees of the British Museum.*
15. Studies for the *Descent from the Cross.* Red chalk, about 1533. *Teyler Museum, Haarlem.*
16. Resurrection. Red chalk, about 1532. Louvre. *Cabinet des Dessins, Musee du Louvre.*

INTRODUCTION

Michelangelo's contemporaries thought him the greatest artist who had ever lived and they called him 'divine'. His repu-
tation as sculptor, architect, painter and draughtsman has
not subsequently been surpassed and who is to say that his
contemporaries were wrong? Their opinion has not dated. He
was, and is, the archetype of genius in the visual arts. He is
also the archetypal *artist* and the central paradox around
which his life revolved is the basis of the mystique which
surrounds that term. That paradox, put simply, is one of
success and failure, the failure of a superhuman achievement
in the light of an even more superhuman ambition. In Michelangelo the man, it showed itself in a profound melancholy
marching step by step with a vast public esteem until the
man, raised to a status of demi-god, found himself forced
further and further out of human intercourse and into an
especial purgatory. Fortuitously but none the less certainly,
it was Michelangelo even more than Raphael and Leonardo
who raised the image-maker from craftsman to artist, that
mysterious state of forlorn grace beyond normality. In doing
so, he changed the attitude of the spectator from one of
simple satisfaction to one of awed disquiet. The fate which
was imposed upon Prometheus for the crime of stealing a coal
of divine fire from Olympus and betraying its secret to mortal
men, caused him to be chained to the summit of a mountain
for thirty or some say thirty thousand years. Furthermore his
liver was perpetually gnawed by an eagle, an insatiable bird

which might perhaps be identified symbolically with a particular kind of self-knowledge. Chained to the summit of the Renaissance for thirty years, the Promethean Michelangelo imposed his chains upon his followers. He took the image-maker and transformed him.

Primitive man did, and in some places still does, make images to gain power over the unknown forces which menace him and over those elements, creatures and conditions of the natural world upon which he depends for survival. His rituals, among them his dance, his song and his painting, are directed towards the conquest of opponents who may be vulnerable, or the propitiation of gods who could make them so. In the course of time these rituals have become enormously diverse but throughout man's prehistory and his history, the impulse towards power has generally been more potent than any other and the practice of image-making is a profound exercise of power. Aesthetics are a by-product of this exercise and aesthetics vary greatly throughout history, not only in their general relevance to image-making but in their importance. Primitive man was perhaps at once priest and image-maker. Society, as it developed, divided the function and subordinated the image-maker to the priest. From Pre-Dynastic Egypt at least until the Reformation the priest dictated the form of the most significant kinds of image; the craftsman followed that dictation as literally as the conventions required. The difference between a painting made as a votive offering to a rain god or to Apollo or to God the Father is not an absolute difference. The sculptured totem of a tribe dedicated to antelopes or of a church dedicated to a saint, remains sculpture motivated by the same kind of impulse. The change that Michelangelo brought about does not alter the basic impulse but adds a further dimension to it. The Promethean situation restores to the craftsman his initial status as priest and he becomes again the shaman, the direct manipulator of power, but the implications are different. The chains of Prometheus hold him captive.

The title of *magister* in medieval and Renaissance times meant 'master' in the sense of a master of skills. It did not mean *artist*. The master required of himself an integrity to his craft in the honourable practise of his skills and although he may have sought to extend their range, the purpose to which those skills were put was specific—as specific as the work required of him. Its success or failure depended upon common consent, or, at least, upon the consent of rulers spiritual and temporal.

If, in their essence, the visual arts were intended to make the unknown visible and knowable and therefore governable, that governance could only be exercised by common consent. From the flattery and propitiation of gods to the flattery and propitiation of princes is a small step and it was taken early. The prestige of princes lay, and has always lain, partially in the excellence of the craftsmen who served them, so that a mutual prestige which lent status to the craftsman and pride to the prince rested naturally upon what the prince and his court deemed excellent. Even this is a mere extension of the function of image-making, since prestige lent power to the prince. Nor has this altered superficially. The prestige of artists still depends upon the consent of customers, but with a subtle and vital difference for which Michelangelo was in some degree responsible. To suggest a parallel, the success of the painter or sculptor, before Michelangelo, was not unlike the success of an actor today. The status of an actor depends specifically upon immediate and common consent and in this his problem remains an external one. It can be tested and measured. His ambition need not lead him further than to perfect his craft in the esteem of his audience and his colleagues. He serves his profession, he serves his public and no Prometheus is necessary in him to hurl any prophecy at Zeus. He has no call to teach a God 'How far from sovereignty is servitude', as Aeschylus put it. This was true of the image-maker before Michelangelo and has often been true since, but it is not true of that creature called *the artist*. Only a master of Promethean stature could, as early as the sixteenth century, have played the Promethean role and earned the first chains. Only a Michelangelo could have earned the initial attention of the eagle and left *the artist*, his every successor, with a predatory chick from that dread bird's egg. For in that egg is a sense of failure which cannot be comforted by applause and a distrust of applause so profound that it is a kind of *hubris*. The lonely figure in the grip of the eagle's claws is the romantic *idea* of *the artist*.

Michelangelo was the first and greatest *artist* in this sense. He was the first man to count himself a failure in the very teeth of the greatest personal success ever won by an image-maker. His failure lay in his ambition and in the distant goal—far beyond the praises of a sequence of popes—he set himself to gain. In striving for it he achieved a level of creation which earned him the title of 'divine' and he explored and made visible an area of experience. He did not, however, make it governable, conquering only a part of it, and even that part only he could govern: it eluded his followers. In that process he initiated a struggle which has since become the norm. The artist dying in squalor, the misunderstood genius, the artist driven mad, the artist ahead of his times, haunted by immeasurable longings, persecuted by philistines, reaching towards the unattainable, trying to 'express himself', all these notions and their catch-phrases are part of this heritage. All of them create a sense of the *artist* as disorientated and this for various complicated reasons, has become increasingly acceptable to us. There is, however, a paradox present in the fact that the romantic conceit feeds on overt if temporary failure—on the passion and tragedy of a Van Gogh—and not upon its exact opposite, the torment of the acknowledged demi-god. It is not so easy to enjoy vicariously the secret sorrows of the 'divine'.

When I suggest that Michelangelo explored the unknown and made it visible in a new aspect, that, in its deepest sense, is no more than the ancient function of the image-maker and I do not wish to suggest that his art was not founded on that of his predecessors. Without the Renaissance of Masaccio and Donatello and the proto-Renaissance of Giotto and Giovanni Pisano, he could not have made the extraordinary thrust into the unknown which he accomplished.

The traditions to which Michelangelo belonged were two and they were at odds. At first glance he grows in the sunlight of the Florentine Renaissance with its noble homage to the ancient world, its open and ordered classicism and that splendid concept called *disegno* which brought drawing to its highest estate; drawing as the definition of structure, as the explanation of form and as the description of volumes. But Michelangelo's tradition was also rooted in the Gothic and it is his Gothic inheritance which enabled him to express, with such splendour, a restless and tormented energy held in ruthless check. His dark sense of martyrdom, of torment by unrealisable aspirations, of that melancholy which regarded life as a transitory thing, have their forerunner in Giovanni Pisano, the greatest of Italian Gothic sculptors, no less than in the puritanism of Savonarola's reaction against Renaissance humanism. Where Michelangelo differs from his every predecessor is in the depth and extent of his introversion. Rodin described Michelangelo as 'the culmination of Gothic thought' who 'celebrated the epic of shadow while the ancients celebrated that of light' and Michelangelo himself speaks of 'walking from dark to dark'.

The central concern of Renaissance art was with the definition of objects, with their *particularity* and their exact appearance, with their shining, apparent, reality. The tangible and actual, revealed in pristine clarity, ordered by geometry, celebrated in light, these are the qualities which the Renaissance shares with ancient Greece. Compare the world of Leonardo da Vinci with the cosmic limbo of Michelangelo. No aspect of the study of natural phenomena escaped Leonardo, from the stratification of rocks to the formation of a spray of bramble, from hydraulics to cartography. No curiosity has ever been more boundless, no researches into the particularity of things has been wider than Leonardo's, but the only point at which Michelangelo and Leonardo meet is in the field of anatomy. The only quality they share is stature.

Nothing is more remote from Michelangelo than this curiosity about specific things. No one rejected the particularities of the world about him more vehemently in his art. Nothing is specific in it except the trunk and limbs of the titanic nude. There is no costume in his painting, only such impersonal drapery as will further explain the action of the limbs beneath it. There are no utensils, there is no still life and no furniture. His people do not live in houses or walk the streets, or ride horses. They do not inhabit a landscape and they are unaffected by the seasons. Where they occupy ground, it is a treeless desert which surrounds them, a bleak platform for activity. No specific portrait from Michelangelo's hand survives, although he is thought to have made a handful of portrait drawings during his seventy-five years of working life. In short, he needed nothing to forward his grand design but the naked human body. As his vision evolves, even the extremities of that body, the fingers and toes of his sculptured figures, sometimes cease to be defined and lose their particularity. The protagonists in his drama take no account either of place or time. Even the definition of sex in Michelangelo's images is equivocal. The male and female distinctions shift disconcertingly and give place to the three elements central to his vision: weight, articulation and thrust. The envelope he evolved for the immeasurable energy which impelled each protagonist is supernormal and totally at odds with the natural realm in which his contemporaries had their being.

Onde dall' arte è vinta la natura proclaims the conquest and overthrow of nature and beyond nature the celebration of forces moved by a will to act without hope of success, of a desperate and restless energy as remote from Olympus as it is from Arcadia.

Antique art, which to Michelangelo meant Hellenistic and Roman sculpture and to which in his youth he paid great attention, was also occasionally subject to this tendency, although never on such a scale. We are inclined to think of Greek sculpture in terms of the Elgin marbles and of earlier works, wherein an ordered proportion aimed at an ideal. We think of a harmony Pater described as the condition wherein 'the thought does not outstrip or lie beyond its sensible embodiment'. This ideal meant nothing to Michelangelo and his 'antiquity' lay in the torment of the Läocoön. He outstripped at every stage the sensible embodiment of the thought and no less the physical possibilities of the human frame in his response to his impulse to subject this fragile human vehicle to extremities of weight, thrust and energy beyond the limits of its articulation. In creating the painted titans of *The Last Judgement* and the unfinished marble 'Slaves', intended for the tomb of Julius II, he brought forth a race of superhumans which rapidly degenerated, in the hands of his followers, Vasari, Giulio Romano, Pellegrino Tibaldi and others, into a race of ludicrous muscle-bound monsters.

In the light of this, the failure of the major sculptural project of his life—the Tomb of Julius II—is important because although this grandiose scheme failed to materialise through no fault of Michelangelo's, less indeed than was the case with the Medici funerary chapel which was also abandoned incomplete, his melancholy obsession with his own inadequacy is connected with the failure of his greatest schemes as a sculptor, and this is expressed most intimately in his verse.

Sculpture is a physical experience different in kind from painting and as a sculptor first and last Michelangelo is concerned with the human body as a plastic entity, that is to say, as a three-dimensional object to be experienced and manipulated as a solid in space. In painting he sought to represent form sculpturally rather than pictorially with the same ends in view. Yet in his verse he practically never refers to the human body, except to the decrepit condition of his own and when he does, he does not deal with it as a tactile thing. On the contrary, *the face* of the beloved and not his or her body is continually in evidence in the sonnets. This is curious in a man who paid so little attention to the particular appearance of people in painting and sculpture that he did not practise the art of portraiture despite its importance in the Renaissance canon. It is also strange that a man whose sacrament in painting and sculpture might be described as an outward and visible sign of an inward *and physical energy*, should dwell at such length in his verse upon the weary frailty of old age and the spiritual implications of platonic love. It is almost as if the poetry of Michelangelo is a complementary aspect of his genius, so exactly is it the reverse of the medal struck by his sculpture and painting.

His verse is confessional. Much of it is a plaint, much of

[16]

it illuminates an almost craven humility and when it celebrates an occasional and short-lived victory over the looming darkness of life, such moments are attributed solely to grace. Where in poetry he enjoys for a moment a fraction of the gigantic exaltation which is at the core of his visual images, he attributes his relief solely to the virtue or beauty of the loved object. He himself is nothing. He walks from dark to dark, 'living on his death'. In the sonnets after the death of Vittoria Colonna and in the last sequences of penitential sonnets, he repeatedly stresses his weakness, his baseness and his total reliance for survival upon forces outside himself. Sonnets LXIV and LXX, for instance, show this abject humility yet they were written by the man whose ferocity and grandeur were famed in the word *Terribilità*, the man whom Pope Leo X called 'Terrifying' and to whom Sebastiano del' Piombo wrote, 'You frighten everyone, even Popes.'

Michelangelo's war within himself, his struggle to survive the Promethean eagle, was, I believe, a struggle to withstand the pressure of his own personality. The twin forces at war, good and evil, god and the devil, the spirit and the flesh, as they may variously be called, may seem to be represented in the artist by a struggle between the impersonal and the personal. The *personality* tends to laud its limitations as positive virtues, whereas the area beyond those limitations can only be gained by the deliberate rejection of the personal in order to overcome or penetrate the limitations. Of this, Michelangelo was plainly aware and the excessive humility and self-abasement of his verse seem to me to show it. The greatness of his painting and sculpture exists paradoxically not in a triumph of 'self expression' but in the reverse, in a triumph over the self, the greater because as the archetypal *artist*, Michelangelo was in fact the image-maker confronted with *himself*. Self knowledge, an overwhelming awareness of the

[17]

self, in the special sense in which I use it here, is opposed to the creative act in the arts, principally because it inhibits the act of identification with the subject, which is essential to the making of potent images. A man who cannot *become* the thing he seeks to portray by an imaginative transference which requires the rejection of himself, cannot truly portray it. In the light of this, Sonnet XXI is no mere poetic conceit. It describes precisely the process necessary to come to terms with the loved object by an act which is at once both one of propitiation and one of conquest.

The majority of Michelangelo's sonnets were written in the last thirty years of his life, that is to say, after he finally settled in Rome in 1534. By this time, Leonardo and Raphael were dead and Michelangelo was without rivals. He was the surviving giant from a golden age, but he was also, in some sort, a refugee from his native city of Florence and from the tyranny of a Medici newly created 'Duke'. As a man without rivals, with Spain, France, Flanders and Venice following his lead and with artists as great as Tintoretto and El Greco in his debt, employed by the fifth in the series of Popes to commission him and about to begin *The Last Judgement* in the Sistine Chapel, he must have seemed to his contemporaries to have arrived at the summit of human ambition. To read the sonnets is to see how little that meant to him, and to follow those last thirty years of his life is to watch a supreme master move towards the lonely and desperate condition of one who is answerable only to himself. And that is to watch a man embark upon a work *which cannot be finished.*

Michelangelo's life before he settled in Rome in 1534 had consisted of a series of triumphs offset by a series of grandiose schemes which remained unrealised for external reasons beyond his control. Ultimately his very last works were to fail, if such a word could be applied to them except by their creator, for internal reasons equally beyond his control. The pattern of triumph and frustration had been constant throughout his life.

Born in 1475 at Caprese in Florentine territory, he had mastered the techniques of painting, in the studio of Domenico Ghirlandaio, by the time he was fourteen. His three years' apprenticeship as a painter was then cut short by Lorenzo de Medici, who set him under the sculptor Bertoldo in the school founded by Lorenzo, in the Medici gardens. By 1496, Michelangelo was in Rome, after an interlude at Bologna, and there carved the *Bacchus* and the first *Pieta*, now in St. Peter's, which made his name. In 1501 he returned to Florence and worked on a number of commissions, including the colossal 'David' adapted with incredible ingenuity from a block of marble botched and abandoned by another sculptor. In 1503 he began a series of twelve marble Apostles for the Cathedral of Florence. They were never completed. In 1504 he made numerous studies and a complete cartoon for a fresco representing an incident in the Pisan war. This fresco was intended for the Council Chamber in the Palazzo Vecchio and was to complement Leonardo's equally ill-fated *Battle of Anghiari*. Michelangelo's cartoon for this painting, the so-called *Cascina Cartoon*, became one of the most influential works of the later Renaissance. It was destroyed during his lifetime. His failure to complete the fresco was caused by the importunate demands of Pope Julius II, and Michelangelo left for Rome to begin the sculptures for a tomb which the Pope was anxious to have completed during his own lifetime. There were to be forty marble sculptures ornamenting the Papal resting place and on this project Michelangelo worked for forty years. It was never completed, although it was the subject of five successive contracts with four successive popes. In 1506 he completed a colossal bronze of Julius II at Bologna. In 1511 it was destroyed. In 1508 he returned to Rome and began to paint the ceiling of the Sistine Chapel, and on this he worked in circumstances of great difficulty, virtually alone, until 1512. How he felt about this undertaking is described in Sonnet V, but at least it was finished. This work, at the age of thirty-seven, earned him the title 'divine'.

Julius II died and the new Pope Leo X was a Medici, the younger son of Lorenzo. He remained Michelangelo's master until his death in 1521, when another Medici became pope, Clement VII, who continued to employ Michelangelo so that it was for the Medici family or for a Medici pope that he worked until 1534. During that time he wasted four years on the façade of S. Lorenzo—which to this day has no façade—and carved the sculptures for the Medici Chapel, which remains incomplete. He also designed the Laurencian Library.

In 1527 the Medici were expelled from Florence and Michelangelo, an ardent republican, took part in the defence of the city until its capitulation in 1530. The Medici were reinstated and Michelangelo was pardoned, but after working for four more years on the sculptures for the Medici Chapel, he left Florence for good. It was the pattern of his life that in painting, an activity of which he thought little, his greatest designs were completed, with the exception of the fresco for the Palazzo Vecchio, whereas in sculpture, which he considered his proper profession, all his greatest projects failed to materialise or remained in some compromise form to mock him. He was the longest lived of the three masters who stand at the summit of the High Renaissance and who together created *the artist* in his new status. The pattern these giants present is one of a strangely blighted perfection, as if the gods had shown their jealousy towards men in the ancient fashion. Michelangelo, as we have seen, saw himself defeated; Leo-

nardo da Vinci watched his grandest achievements destroyed
or perish; Raphael failed in nothing, but he died at only
thirty-seven. The defeat of Leonardo, if it can be so described,
might be called the result of a divine carelessness, of an im-
patience so profound and a restless curiosity so deep that specific achievement meant little to him. Michelangelo's nemesis
was a divine discontent so high and terrible that specific
achievement was forever unattainable. In his latest carvings,
when he was working solely for himself and for his God,
nothing is finished, but in many much earlier works he deliberately left his marbles rough and 'unfinished' as compared
to those of his contemporaries. The 'Slaves' emerge ambigu-
ously from the marble as if man remained forever embedded
in a primeval matrix. What remained unresolved in the sculptures for the tomb of Julius as certainly the fortuitous result of circumstance and the normal frustrations inherent in
contracts drawn up with princes and popes, but there is also
an enigma beyond simple circumstance, an unanswerable
question posed as to whether or not Michelangelo recognised
implicitly that these sculptures would not and could not, of
their nature, come to completion.

Carving is the slowest and the most laborious of the arts.
'By sculpture,' Michelangelo said, 'I understand an art which
operates by taking away superfluous material; by painting one
that attains its results by laying on.' Michelangelo therefore
sought to release his vision from the core of stone but as
his wisdom and pessimism increased, the definition of his
vision became increasingly uncertain. Inevitably the doubts
which develop from this huge uncertainty as to the nature
of truth, create a condition in which it becomes impossible to
know *what material is superfluous* and from this must follow
the suspicion that all material may be superfluous. In this
dilemma, I suspect, Michelangelo dwelt at the very end of his

[21]

life and perhaps it explains the last and strangest of all his sculptures and the four final lines of his poetry (LXXVIII), where he describes a final identification with the material from which he had wrought his life. The sacrament of Michelangelo had grown from the outward and physical sign of a gigantic inward and physical energy into the outward and barely physical sign of an inward and spiritual grace.

Although the forms in his last drawings are palpable and dense, they seem to emerge from a mist of hazarded contours. It is as if he had begun to build back the matrix round the core of his vision. They are drawings which lie in an area of experience only dimly perceptible to the spectator but they still emanate restless power. In contrast, the *Rondanini Pieta* is a statue so stripped, so bare, so passive and so patient that all the spent strength of the titan is drained away and only the spirit remains within a slim and fragile shell of stone.

It is possible that the resignation embodied in this extraordinary carving derives from a reconciliation with the most relentless and immediate of Michelangelo's three judges? There are only three who can sit in judgement upon a man so exalted by genius above his fellow men and their institutions. One is Time—and we know Time's judgement of Michelangelo. One is God, who does not pronounce judgement until time stops. The third is the man himself and the sonnets describe the terrible harshness of that judgement in Michelangelo's case. On the 12th of February 1564 he worked, standing all day, at this last *Pieta*, drastically recutting the stone so that it remains now in a state of transition between two quite different conceptions of the same subject. A disembodied arm remains to testify to the first vision, as does the first version of the Virgin's face, upturned and left like a ghost upon the headdress of her bowed head. The Dead Christ, slim and worn as a sea-washed bone, is as remote from the all-conquering athlete of *The Last Judgement* as sleep is from earthquake. The thrust is gone, the weight is gone, the articulation no longer describes energy.

In the *Rondanini Pieta* is the still centre. The trembling mountains, the turbid seas and the fallen angels of which he speaks in sonnet LXXVI may seem to surround the spectator; they do not touch the sculpture. It is unfinished and it is finished. Six days later, on February 18th, it was all finished. Michelangelo was dead. He was eighty-nine years old.

1. STUDY FOR ONE OF THE THREE MAGI

2. & 3. STUDIES OF A HORSE AND A BATTLE SCENE

WITH DRAFTS OF FOUR POEMS AND SONNET III

4. YOUTH WITH LEFT ARM EXTENDED

A NOTE ON THE ILLUSTRATIONS

There is no specific connection between any surviving drawing by Michelangelo and any of his sonnets. He did not illustrate his poems and the fact that there are sonnets on the Crucifixion and sonnets in which sculpture occurs as an image does not relate individual drawings to individual poems. The plates in this edition are an anthology chosen to represent various aspects of the artist's style and to coincide in character with the mood of the poems. The drawings do not relate in date to the putative dating of the sonnets, most of which seem to have been written after 1534 but cover a wider range of Michelangelo's working life. Furthermore there is much disagreement among authorities as to the dating of individual drawings.

There are, however, certain studies which are fortuitously connected with the verse. Of these, the sketches of a horse and a battle scene are included because on this sheet, Pl. 3 and 4, Michelangelo has jotted down drafts of four poems and a complete draft of Sonnet III. Pl. 5 and 6 are studies for the Sistine Chapel ceiling and the Tomb of Julius II and therefore bear a relation to sonnets III, IV and V, which deal with these subjects. In like manner, Pl. 9 and 10 are included because the first was presented to Gherardo Perini by the artist and the second is a study for 'The Fall of Phaeton' which was given to Tomasso de Cavalieri and both these young men, together with Febo del Poggio and Cecchino Bracci, were objects of Michelangelo's love. Several sonnets

[25]

are dedicated to Cavalieri and there is documentary evidence that Michelangelo made a portrait drawing of him and one of Cecchino Bracci. Both are lost. Pl. 15, a carefully finished drawing in Michelangelo's 'presentation' style, was made expressly for Vittoria Colonna. This noble and pious lady whose friendship with Michelangelo was of the highest importance to him in his latter years, was a poet much admired in her time and one whose religious views were highly sympathetic to Michelangelo. The extent of his love for her is shown in the sonnets dedicated to her and those which mourn her death. The drawing of the Crucifixion which survives from among several made for Vittoria Colonna, is remarkable in that it presents the Crucified Christ as alive and suffering with upcast head and eyes. This is in direct opposition to the Renaissance tradition which represents him dead and Mediæval tradition which portrays him alive but triumphant. It was much copied and engraved and became the prototype of later crucifixions not only in Italy but elsewhere and El Greco, Reni, Rubens and Van Dyck were among those who adopted this convention.

TRANSLATOR'S NOTE

My chief endeavour in producing metrical versions of these poems has been to retain the sense and meaning and, at the same time, to attempt some sort of rhythmic pattern which is not too far from the form and spirit of the originals. It is always difficult to make a translation from an inflected language into an uninflected one; and where the poems in question are sonnets with a rigid rhyme-scheme, the task is even more complex. I have made no attempt to preserve the exact rhyme-scheme of these sonnets because to do so would have demanded too great a sacrifice of meaning and content.

As for the thought in these poems—it is not only often metaphysical but sometimes positively baffling. Michelangelo set great store by compression and it has sometimes been necessary to simplify his argument in order that the poem may be more accessible to the modern reader. Nowhere, however, has the meaning been deliberately suppressed or altered.

Michelangelo's rhetoric and theology are unfashionable to-day. Yet, as in the poems of Donne and Hopkins, the sense of struggle in his sonnets, the feeling of passion just within control, can hardly fail to move and excite the contemporary reader of poetry. These sonnets are, I think, not unlike Michelangelo's sculpture. In both media, the dominating feature is vehement energy, an energy which is mastered by a longing for order.

To read the sonnets sensitively is, I believe, to gain an

insight into Michelangelo's mind which will illuminate our approach to his sculpture and painting. He wears no masks in these poems and presents no superficial *persona*. I hope that my rendering of the poems will have preserved at least something of the poignant experiences of a noble and tormented man.

My most grateful thanks are due to Lt. Cdr. John Folger R.N. who has made my task so much easier by providing me with English prose translations of Michelangelo's sonnets.

ELIZABETH JENNINGS

THE SONNETS
OF
MICHELANGELO

I

ON DANTE ALIGHIERI

From heaven he came, in mortal clothing, when
All that was worst and best had been observed.
Living, he came to view the God he served
To give us the entire, true light again.

For that bright star which with its vivid rays
Picked out the humble place where I was born—
For this, the world would be a prize to scorn;
None but its Maker can return its praise.

I speak of Dante, he whose work was spurned
By the ungrateful crowd, those who can give
Praise only to the worthless. I would live

Happy were I but he, by such men scorned,
If, with his torments, I could also share
His greatness, both his joy and exile bear.

II

It is not possible to say how much
We owe to him, because his splendour blinds
Our eyes. Simpler it is to blame those minds
Too small to honour him, to sense his touch.

He did not fear to plumb to places where
Failure alone survives. But this was done
For our example. Always he was near
To God. Only his country dared to shun

His greatness. Her ingratitude at last
Turned on herself. As proof of this, observe
How always to the perfect sorrows fall

Most painfully. To those who are the best
Most ill occurs. Dante did not deserve
Exile; his equal never lived at all.

III

My Lord, of all the ancient proverbs, this
Is surely true—"Who can doth never will".
You have believed in saws and promises
And blest those men whom falsehoods, not truths, fill.

Always I have been faithful and would give
Honour to you as rays do to the sun.
Yet all my pain has never made you grieve,
The less I please, the more work I have done.

Once I had hoped to climb by means of your
Great height, but now I find we rather need
Justice and power, not echoes faint indeed.

Heaven, it appears, itself is made impure
When worldliness has power. I live to take
Fruit from a tree too dry to bear or break.

IV

Here they make helms and swords from chalices;
The blood of Christ is sold now by the quart.
Lances and shields are shaped from thorns and crosses,
Yet still Christ pours out pity from his heart.

But let him come no more into these streets
Since it would make his blood spurt to the stars;
In Rome they sell his flesh, and virtue waits
Helpless, while evil every entrance bars.

If ever I desired reward, oh now
All chance is gone. My work has come to naught.
Medusa hides beneath that mantle there.

Heaven rewards poverty, but here below
What chance have we to find the good we sought
When men are false to the great signs they bear?

TO GIOVANNI DA PISTOJA
ON THE PAINTING OF THE SISTINE CHAPEL

Like cats from Lombardy and other places
Stagnant and stale, I've grown a goitre here;
Under my chin my belly will appear,
Each the other's rightful stance displaces.

My beard turns heavenward, my mind seems shut
Into a casket. With my breast I make
A shield. My brush moves quickly, colours break
Everywhere, like a street mosaic-cut.

My loins are thrust into my belly and
I use my bottom now to bear the weight
Of back and side. My feet move dumb and blind.
In front my skin is loose and yet behind
It stretches taut and smooth, is tight and straight.

I am a Syrian bow strained for the pull—
A hard position whence my art may grow.
Little, it seems, that's strong and beautiful

Can come from all the pains I undergo.
Giovanni, let my dying art defend
Your honour, in this place where I am left
Helpless, unhappy, even of art bereft.

VI

INVECTIVE AGAINST THE PEOPLE OF PISTOJA

I *have received your word now twenty times,*
Read it as many. May it do you good.
As little, I hope, as teeth can do for food
When stomach aches and indigestion climbs.

Now I know certainly that evil Cain
Was your own ancestor. You do again
What he and all his followers did. What good
They had has gone with your ingratitude.

Proud you are, envious, enemies of heaven,
Friends to your own harm and, to your own neighbour,
The simplest charity you find a labour.

See, to Pistoja Dante's curse was given.
Remember that if good words you say
Of Florence, you but wish to wheedle me.

A jewel far beyond all price is she.
This is a thing you cannot comprehend:
It takes real virtue thus to understand.

VII

TO LUIGI DEL RICCIO

It happens sometimes even in the great
Sweetness of courtesy, of life and honour,
That an offence can hide. Thus, in this manner
Some good is spoilt and mars my healthy state.

He who can give to others wings of hope
Yet stretch a hidden net along their way,
Is false to the great fire of charity
And brings true friendship to a sudden stop.

Therefore, keep clear, Luigi, that first grace
To which I owe my life, let no storm mar
Its calm, let not wind stir its steady peace.

Contempt can make all gratitude obscure,
But, with true friendship, nothing can displace
Its strength. For this, pain is a way to please.

VIII

I scarcely knew him when his eyes were shut
For ever, he who was your life and light.
His eyes closed fast at death's last parting, but
Opened on God and found a love more bright.

I know and weep; yet it was not my fault
That I should meet him too late to admire
His grace. Your memory becomes his vault,
Lost not to you, only to my desire.

Then if, Luigi, I must carve the form
Of him, Cecchino, whom I speak about,
And change him from this dust to living stone,

You, his friend, must keep his image warm,
And if you fail, my art is called in doubt.
I'll find his likeness now in you alone.

IX

Your gifts—the sugar, candles and the mule,
Also the cask of Malmsey wine—so far
Exceed necessity, I must defer
Thanks to St. Michael, let him tip the scale.

Like weather in a calm, prosperity
Can make sails drop. Thus my frail barque seems lost
Amid a raging, wild and cruel sea;
Like a soft feather, it is tempest-tossed.

As for your kindness and your gifts, for all
The food and drink, the journeys to and fro,
Which for my need and pleasure have been set—

Dear Lord, I cannot pay you what I owe;
To give you all I have would be to fail
Because it is no gift to pay a debt.

X

TO GANDOLFO PORRINO
ON HIS MISTRESS FAUSTINA MANCINA

Unique in heaven as on this wicked earth
(Though cheaply by the vulgar crowd is she
Named—that crowd, too blind to see her worth),
The new high beauty was designed to be

For you alone. Neither with tools nor pen
Would I know how to fashion her or trace
The radiant beauty of her living face.
For that, you must return to life again.

And if she overwhelms imagination
As the great sun outshines the other stars,
Still you may rate her at her real price.

To calm your pining and your desolation
God moulds her beauty which can far surpass
All I can make. My art will not suffice.

XI

With pen and colours you have shown how art
Can equal nature. Also in a sense
You have from nature snatched her eminence,
Making the painted beauty touch the heart.

Now a more worthy work your skilful hand,
Writing on paper, labours and contrives—
To give to those who're dead new worth, new lives;
Where nature simply made, you understand.

When men have tried in other centuries
To vie with nature in the power to make,
Always they had to yield to her at last.

But you, illuminating memories,
Bring back to life these lives for their own sake,
And conquer nature with the vivid past.

XII

Oh happy spirit, who with so much zeal
Remembers me though I am soon to die.
Among so many other joys you feel
The wish to greet me. What great loyalty!

You, who delighted me when I could see
Your face, now comfort me within my mind.
You bring new hope to all my misery
That old desires will always leave behind.

Finding in you a willingness to plead
My cause, although you have so many cares,
He who now writes returns you thanks for this.

It would be shame and usury to press
These ugly pictures on you when I need
To bring to life again your loveliness.

XIII

TO THE SAME

To be more worthy of you, Lady, is
My sole desire. For all your kindnesses
I try to show, with all I have of art,
And courtesy, the gladness of my heart.

But well I know that simply by my own
Efforts I cannot match your goodness. Then
I ask your pardon for what's left undone,
And failing thus, I grow more wise again.

Indeed, I know it would be wrong to hope
That favours, raining from you as from heaven,
Could be repaid by human work so frail.

Art, talent, memory, with all their scope
Can never pay you back what you have given.
At this, a thousand tries would always fail.

XIV(i)

Whenever perfect works of art are planned,
The craftsman always makes a model to
Be the first simple part from which shall grow
The finished object underneath his hand.

Later, in living stone, more perfect still,
A lovelier thing is shaped; beneath the blows
Of the fierce hammer, he can feel the thrill
Of art emerging from its own birth throes.

So was I born as my own model first,
The model of myself; later would I
Be made more perfect, born of one so high.

If all my roughness, then, should be so blest
By your compassion, then what penance ought
My feverish ardour by your rules be taught?

XIV(ii)

If noble concepts have a birth divine
In human looks and acts, the value is
Doubled—that from such petty images
A face, not art's, should in the dull stone shine.

Likewise on roughest paper, artists will
Make sketches, long before they use the brush.
Among a hundred efforts, crude and rash,
The right one springs at last from so much skill.

And so with me, among all models least:
For I was born to a great destiny—
To find new birth in you, Lady most high,

If all my roughness, then, should be so blest
By your compassion, then what penance ought
My feverish ardour by your rules be taught?

XV

The marble not yet carved can hold the form
Of every thought the greatest artist has,
And no conception can yet come to pass
Unless the hand obeys the intellect.

The evil that I fly from, all the harm,
The good also, are buried and intact
In you, proud Lady. To my life's sad loss
My art's opposed to the desired effect.

Thus love, and your own beauty and the weight
Of things, are not to blame for my own plight.
Fate, scorn or chance can never be accused

Because both death and pity are enclosed
Within your heart, and I have only breath
And power to draw from you not life but death.

XVI

Just as in pen and ink, the high and low
And mediocre styles can find expression,
And as in marbles the imagination,
Noble or base, will its own worth bestow;

So, my dear Lord, whatever finds its place
Within your heart—pride or humility—
I draw from it only what moves in me,
As you can tell from what shows on my face.

For he who sows both sighs and tears will find
(Since heaven, whose dew is always pure and clear,
To different seeds will variously appear),

That what he reaps is sorrow. Heart and mind,
When grievously afflicted, still will see
In greatest beauty only misery.

XVII

Lady, how can it be that what is shown
Through long experience and imagination
Endures so long in hard and mountain stone,
While years enact the maker's consummation?

The cause to the effect yields and gives place,
Nature by art is overcome at last.
I know too well who work with sculptor's grace
That time and death resign me to the past.

Thus can I give long life to you and me
In one way, either in stone or else in paint
Which seems to show each other's faces true.

Thus, in a thousand years all men shall see
How beautiful you were, how I was faint
And yet how wise I was in loving you.

5. STUDY FOR THE MEDICI TOMBS

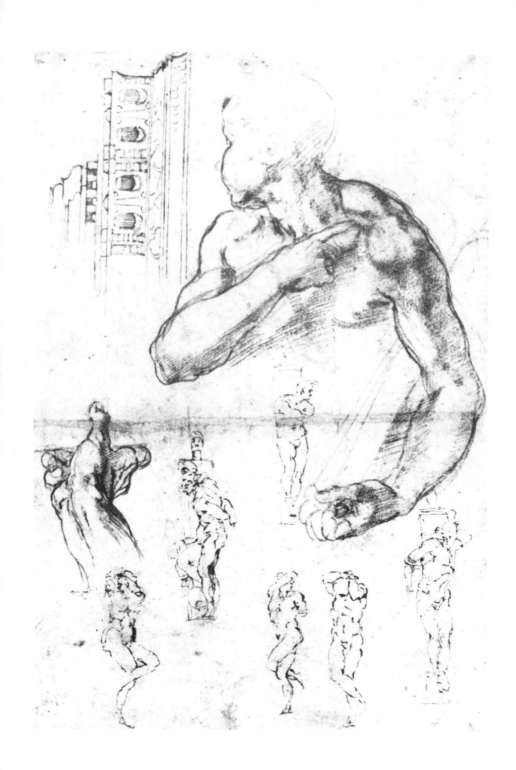

6. STUDIES FOR THE SISTINE CHAPEL CEILING
AND THE TOMB OF JULIUS II

7. UNFINISHED STUDY OF A HEAD

8. VIRGIN AND CHILD WITH ST. ANNE

XVIII

With heart of sulphur and with flesh of tow,
With bone designed of dry and rotting wood,
With spirit lacking any guide to show
Which impulses are evil and which good,

With reason which displays itself so weak
Confronted with a world so full of snares,
It is no wonder that my flesh should break
When it first stumbles on such furious fires.

With glorious art—that gift received from heaven—
That conquers nature and in every way
Clings to all human longing and desire;

If such a gift I truly have been given
And yet, divided, torn, still burn and stray,
He is to blame who fashioned me for fire.

XIX

More precious am I to myself than ever
I used to be, since you possessed my heart,
Just as the stone that's chiselled by the carver
Has far more value than in its rough state.

Or as a card or paper is more scanned
When sketched upon than when left blank and plain.
Such is my state since I became the end
Of your attention, nor do I complain.

Always I am secure with such a seal,
Like one who carries arms or charms with him
And finds that every peril has grown less.

Against both fire and water I prevail
And with your sign light everything that's dim.
My spit makes pure all that's most poisonous.

XX

How much a garland pleases when it lies,
Woven with flowers, upon some golden hair;
It seems as if each blossom thrusts and tries
To be the first to kiss that forehead fair.

Contented all day long that garment is
Which spreads itself but first clings to her breast.
The golden thread asks nothing but to rest,
Touching her cheeks and throat with tenderness.

More honoured still that ribbon which can lie,
Gilded and shaped in the most cunning fashion,
Touching the breast which it so carefully laces.

And that small belt that knots so easily
Seems to declare, 'Unceasing my caresses.'
Would that my arms might join in such a passion!

XXI

To others merciful and only to
Itself unkind, this lowly creature who
Sloughs off its skin in pain that it may give
Pleasure to others, dies that they may live.

So do I long for such a destiny—
That from my death, my Lord, you might alone
Take life; then by my death I too might be
Changed like the worm which casts its skin on stone.

For if that skin were mine I could at least
Be woven in a gown to clasp that breast,
And so embrace the beauty which I crave.

Then would I gladly die. Or could I save
My Lord's feet from the rain by being shoes
Upon his feet—this also would I choose.

XXII

If in the face, if in the gazing eyes,
The human heart indeed can be observed—
I have no other sign, this must suffice
To show, Lord, what my deep faith has deserved.

Your strength will give me more fidelity,
I trust, for you can see the honest fire
Which does consume me now and begs your pity.
Abundant grace will answer my desire.

Happy the day if this indeed is true!
May time and hours a moment then stand still,
May day and sun pause in their ancient track.

That, not through anything that I may do,
My dear, desired Lord my arms may fill—
His greatness making up for all I lack.

XXIII

Both near and far my eyes can see your face
Wherever it appears. When you are near,
Let your demeanour shy and quiet appear,
And walk with hands held both together close.

The intellect, being untrammelled, pure,
Can through the eyes attain true liberty;
All your great beauty it can clearly see;
Not so the flesh, so vulnerable and poor.

So hard it is to trace an angel's flight
Since we are wingless. We can only praise
And glory in the momentary sight.

If you are both in heaven and with us here,
Make of my flesh a single eye to gaze,
And let no part of me uncouth appear.

XXIV

Well-born spirit, in whom we see reflected
All that is noble in man's character.
How much by heaven and nature is effected
When nothing mars what they have made so clear.

Spirit of grace, in which we put our trust
With inward faith, since on your face appear
Love, pity, kindness, qualities so rare
That seldom with such beauty are they blest.

Love casts a spell and beauty has a hold
Unbreakable upon my eager heart.
Pity and kindness rule me with their glances.

What government or custom in the world,
What cruelty in time or random chances,
Would not from death set such a face apart?

XXV

'Tell me, I beg, Love, if my eyes indeed
See all the truth of beauty which I claim,
Or if I have within me now the same
Power to see all the beauty that I need?

You ought to know the answer since you came
With her to break my peace, disturb my rest.
I would not let the smallest sigh be lost
For such a love, nor ask a lesser flame.'

'The beauty that you see is truly hers,
But as it grows it rises higher still
If through the eyes it reaches to the soul.

Here it becomes divine and beautiful,
And on a mortal thing it now confers
An immortality your eyes to fill.'

XXVI

Grace, Lady, equally with sorrow may
Cause death. A man condemned to mortal pain
May find a sudden pardon sets him free
When long past hope and cold in every vein.

Likewise, your kindness which so far exceeds
My worth, so far surpasses all my needs,
Can cheer my misery with such compassion
That life itself reaches its consummation.

Death can be found in news bitter and sweet,
For joy and sorrow both possess the power
To fill the heart or tighten it too much.

Your beauty has a power just as great;
Then curb it lest my life should fail before
A gift that overwhelms my feeble clutch.

XXVII

I cannot shape an image or acquire,
Either from shadow or from earthly skin,
A counterpart to lessen my desire:
Such armour is your beauty shut within.

Obsessed and moved by you, I seem to get
Weaker. My passion takes my strength away.
By trying to diminish grief I but
Double it. Like death, it comes to stay.

And it is useless now for me to try
To win the race against such loveliness,
Which far outstrips the fastest runner here.

Love with its hands so tenderly will dry
My tears and make all labour seem most dear.
He is no coward who discovers this!

XXVIII

The living portion of my love is not
My heart; the love with which I love has no
Heart, for in human hearts things mean and low
Always exist, in impulse or in thought.

Love which came, like the soul, from God's own hands
Made me without eyes, made you full of light;
That light cannot be seen in what death ends—
The mortal part which hurts me with delight.

Just as from fire the heat cannot be parted,
Neither can I be separated from
That Beauty in whose likeness she is made.

Ardent, I run to joys which cannot fade,
That paradise where your own beauty started,
Eternal loveliness from which you came.

XXIX

The first day I beheld so much unique
Beauty, I trusted that I might be one
Who, like the eagle soaring to the sun,
Finds such a radiance makes its own eyes weak.

The fault was mine; I knew that I had failed,
Since he who follows angels and lacks wings
Is sowing seed on stone, his words are whirled
Away by wind; God takes his questionings.

My heart will not support me when I know
So great a beauty's near; my eyes grow blind
Though, from a distance, it persuades me still.

What will become of me? What guide will show
Some value in myself I yet may find?
When near, you burn me, when far off, you kill.

XXX

This glorious light I see with your own eyes
Since mine are blind and will not let me see.
Your feet lend me their own security
To carry burdens far beyond my size.

Supported by your wings I now am sped,
And by your spirit to heaven I am borne.
According to your will, I'm pale or red—
Hot in the harshest winter, cold in the sun.

All my own longings wait upon your will,
Within your heart my thoughts find formulation,
Upon your breath alone my words find speech.

Just as the moon owes its illumination
To the sun's light, so I am blind until
To every part of heaven your rays will reach.

XXXI

Why, more than ever, do I give such vent
To my desire, when neither tears nor words
Can change the destiny I move towards?
Nothing I do can my own fate prevent.

Why does the weary heart make death appear
Desirable, since every man must die?
There is no consolation for me here
Where joy is far outweighed by misery.

Yet if the blows must come decreed by fate
And I am powerless, there's comfort in
The thought that nothing now can intervene.

If to be blest I must accept defeat
It is no wonder if, alone and nude,
I am by one in arms chained and subdued.

XXXII

If love is chaste, if pity comes from heaven,
If fortune, good or ill, is shared between
Two equal loves, and if one wish can govern
Two hearts, and nothing evil intervene:

If one soul joins two bodies fast for ever
And if, on the same wings, these two can fly,
And if one dart of love can pierce and sever
The vital organs of both equally:

If both love one another with the same
Passion, and if each other's good is sought
By both, if taste and pleasure and desire

Bind such a faithful love-knot, who can claim,
Either with envy, scorn, contempt or ire,
The power to untie so fast a knot?

XXXIII(i)

So *that your beauty may not lose its power,*
I *pray that nature now herself may gather*
All that she gave you once, and bring together
Those lovely things that leave you hour by hour.

May nature then restore to you the grace
That you owned formerly, but may it be
Celestial beauty now which lights your face
And shows your tenderness and charity.

May nature also treasure all my sighs
And hoard my scattered tears, that she may give
Such things to those who love the one I loved.

Thus in another age the man who tries
To win her, may by my own tears be moved
And find in all I lost the power to live.

XXXIII(ii)

In order that your beauties may endure
And triumph over time which takes away,
I hope that nature may again restore
All that slips slowly from you day by day.

And may these things be handed over to
A happier life and fate. Thus in the place
Of attributes that brought such pain to you,
May there shine forth a peaceful, heavenly grace.

Willing I am that heaven should keep my sighs
And hoard my scattered tears to hand them over
To him who loves the one that I have loved.

Thus in another age the man who tries
To win her may by my sharp grief be moved
And in my loss a greater strength discover.

XXXIV

Eternal fire is kindly to cold stone
And draws strength from it. And though stone may fall
To ashes, it has never really gone
But lives in fire and is not lost at all.

And if, in furnaces, through every season
It lasts, it has achieved a higher place,
Just as a purged soul moves from its own prison
And flies to heaven adorned with every grace.

It is the same with me when fierce desires
Reduce me to pale ashes, dry and cold:
I am not lost but find new life indeed.

If I can rise from ashes which seem dead
And come unscathed from these consuming fires,
I am not forged from iron but from gold.

XXXV

This fire, which burns me fiercely and consumes,
Illuminates her face with lights that freeze;
I find a strength in two frail, graceful arms
Which move great weights though they stay motionless.

Matchless spirit! I only understand
That you, so full of life, can yet cause death,
That you, unfettered, yet can bind me with
Chains; you, my only hope, can still offend.

How can it be, my Lord, that beauty has
Such opposite effects, that harm can spring
From one who has no wish to wound or hurt?

Where is my happy life and everything
That had the power to satisfy? She is
Like sun which heats though it is cold at heart.

XXXVI

If the immortal longing which inspires
The thoughts of others can coax my desires,
Perhaps this longing may, in the same fashion,
Give to the tyrant lord of love compassion.

But since the heavenly ordinance disposes
A short life for the flesh, long for the soul,
Sense in itself never quite discloses
Those qualities which are invisible.

Oh then, alas, how can a love that's chaste
(Such as burns now so strongly within me),
Be seen by him whose love is otherwise?

My happy days are ruined and disgraced
Because my lord pays heed to falsity;
If he believes this, then he also lies.

XXXVII

If someone has been favoured with a great
Kindness—they have, perhaps, been saved from death—
What quality can honour such a debt
Which he who owes may find his freedom with?

Yet if such payment could indeed be made,
He who accomplished it would feel some lack,
For when a debt we owe is fully paid
It seems as if we give the favours back.

Therefore, in order to maintain your grace,
Lady, I will myself deliberately
Covet not kindness but ingratitude.

And for this reason I have chosen thus:
Between two equal loves no rule can be.
I want not partnership but servitude.

XXXVIII

Give to my eyes a natural stream or spring,
Not that great wave which raises you so high
Above a level that is customary.
Such weary labour's an unnatural thing.

And you, thick air, that temper to my sight
Celestial radiance, give back to me
My sighs and tears and all my misery;
Strangely your dark face makes my vision bright.

May earth yield up my footsteps that once more
The grass may sprout where it was torn away;
Let echoes which were deaf return my cries.

Beloved, may your glances now restore—
That I may love elsewhere—light to my eyes,
For I know well you are displeased with me.

XXXIX

Reason is sympathetic when I claim
To find in love a lasting happiness.
With strong examples and true words, my shame
Reminds me of the weakness I possess.

She says, 'The living sun can only give
Death, not a phoenix, now to one like you.'
He who himself has no desire to live,
No hands can save, however willing to.

I understand the truth and know my fate:
I have another heart which cruelly
Kills me the more I yield to its demands.

It is between two deaths that my lord stands.
One baffles me, the other one I hate.
In such suspense body and soul will die.

XL(i)

I know not if it is the longed-for night
Of its first maker that the spirit feels,
Or if some old and honoured memory steals
The heart and makes its beauty shine so bright;

Or maybe fame or dreams themselves can bring
A lovely object to the eyes and heart.
From such a vision many tears can spring
And many memories remain to hurt.

I know not what I feel or seek, or who
Guides me, or where I should true guidance seek,
And yet I feel that someone points the way.

This is my state, my Lord, since I saw you;
Both bitterness and sweetness now can sway
My heart. You are the reason I am weak.

9. VENUS, MARS AND CUPID

10. FALL OF PHAETON

11. STUDY OF A HEAD FOR *Leda*

12. WRESTLERS

XL(ii)

I know not if it is imagination
Which makes the light that every man can feel,
Or if from mind or memory will steal
Some other glorious illumination.

Or maybe in the soul the scorching fire
Of heaven still burns, and has the power to draw
Our thoughts into an ardent, fierce desire
For truth itself, the one compelling law.

Oh may I always search for what is true
Although, without a guide, this fire I seek.
Yet still I feel that someone points the way.

Lady, this is my state since I saw you;
Both bitterness and sweetness now can sway
My heart. You are the reason I am weak.

XLI

He who from nothing made all things ordained
That time in two parts should be severed; one
He handed over to the mighty sun,
The other with the nearer moon remained.

From this event, fortune and fate sprang forth,
Mischance or happiness to each man fell.
To me sent the dark time, I know well,
For it has always been with me since birth.

And like all things which make a counterfeit
Of their own nature, so I make my fate
More black by feeling full of pain and grief.

Oh then it is a comfort to find one,
Like you, whose fate is always in the sun,
And share some part of what is your whole life.

XLII

Each shuttered room and every covered place,
Whatever they are made of, hold the night.
The day exists where the sun leaps and plays,
Distributing its full and generous light.

But if night can indeed be overcome
By fire or flame, even a glow-worm may
Conquer her as effectively as day;
One little light can break her powerful gloom.

The open land, where seeds and plants allow
The sun to give them light and life, can be
Broken and hurt by the encroaching plough.

Only in darkness can men fully be
Themselves, and therefore night is holier than
Day; no plant has half the worth of man.

XLIII

Since Phoebus does not stretch his shining hands
Around this cold, soft globe, men tend to say
That night holds all that no-one understands,
The great enigma following the day.

She is so weak that one small, simple glare
Cast by a torch can take her life away;
She is so foolish that a musket may
Smash her whole being with its shot and flare.

If one must find a name for such as she,
Then call her daughter of the sun and earth—
The one holds shade, the other fashions it.

The truth remains—for no praise is she fit
Who is so dull and lacking in all mirth,
And, for the firefly, can feel jealousy.

XLIV

Oh night, oh sweetest time although obscure,
All things you consummate with your own peace.
He who understands and has a clear
Vision of you, honours you, knowing this.

You carry every weary thought away,
You make it possible for peace to grow;
From lowest things to highest, you convey
Me in my dreams to where I want to go.

Shadow of death, for whom all sufferings pause,
At whose arrival every sorrow goes,
Comfort of the afflicted at the last:

You strengthen our weak flesh and make it whole,
You dry our tears and rest the weary soul,
And from the just man snatch the painful past.

XLV

When a lord thrusts his servant into prison
And binds him in cruel chains, that man will be,
After some time, reluctant to be free,
So used will he become to the oppression.

Custom still keeps the tiger, lion and snake
Under restraint; some limits must be set.
The inexperienced artist too must make
Redoubled efforts with much toil and sweat.

But fire does not behave in such a way,
Since if it is extinguished by green wood
It still can warm and nourish an old man.

Then love, like youth's green sap, urges him on
And all the world seems glorious and good
And he is full of boyish energy.

That man who scoffs and says there should be shame
When old men love—that man profanes and lies.
It is no sin when human creatures dream
Of natural loveliness; no sins arise
As long as prudence keeps its sovereign claim.

XLVI

If a small, steady flame can quickly dry
The sap within a young green heart, what power
Will raging bonfires have when they but try
An old man's heart that moves to its last hour?

If time in general gives a meagre span
To life with all its values and its claims,
How much less will it grant a dying man
Who, in old age, still plays at lovers' games?

The answer lies in my experience:
The wind which blows my ashes far away
Deprives the worms of their own rightful prey.

If in green youth I wept at milder pains,
In flames more fierce I've little hope that I
May overwhelm them now my wood is dry.

XLVII

If any fire could equal the great light
Of your own eyes from which I part with sorrow,
The world itself contains no part that might
Not be consumed as by a flaming arrow.

But heaven, tender to our weakness, takes
The power of sight from us and with it all
The beauty which you share; and thus she makes
This bitter, mortal life more bearable.

Beauty and passion are not equal then,
For only that deep centre of the heart
That falls in love, with heaven has any part.

So in my age, this happens, Lord, again:
Because for you I do not burn or die,
Blame not my love but human frailty.

XLVIII

Though long delay breeds greater tenderness
Than our desires in youth can ever know,
Still I regret my love's belatedness—
That passion has so short a time to go.

Heaven is perverse indeed if in its care
For us it still can set old hearts on fire.
This is the fate I must accept and bear—
To love a woman with a sad desire.

Yet may be when the sun sinks in the west
And end of day is reached, I can at least
Be in the greater dark a single shade.

If love has come to me when life must fade,
If I desire, though death must touch me soon,
Oh, of my sunset, Lady, make my noon!

XLIX

From gloomy laughter and delicious tears,
From everlasting to a short-lived peace,
I've lapsed indeed. When truth breeds silences
Then sense is sovereign over truth's affairs.

I cannot say whence these misfortunes come,
Whether from me or from your face. I know
The pains are easier the more they grow.
What heaven are your piercing eyes snatched from?

Your loveliness was never meant to die,
But wrought in heaven to be released among
Men on the earth. Thus I exhausted lie,

Yet find more comfort than when close to you.
If God indeed has planned my death, then who,
When I must die, dare say that you were wrong?

L

Too late I realized that from your soul
I might, much like the phoenix in the sun,
Have warmed myself and been made strong and whole;
So often, in old age, this can be done.

What's swifter than the leopard, lynx or stag
After their prey or flying from a snare?
I could have run once, now I only lag
After the good things I've discovered here.

And yet there is no reason now to grieve
Since in this matchless angel I perceive
My health, my rest and true serenity.

When I was young I should less easily
Have found this joy. Now, when it flies away,
I follow after with much less delay.

LI(i)

Now give me back that time when love was held
On a lose rein, making my passion free.
Return that calm, angelic face to me,
That countenance which every virtue filled.

Bring back those frequent journeys, swift before,
But now so slow to one who's full of years.
Give to my breast the waters and the fires
If you require my service any more.

If you can only live upon the tide
Of bitter-sweet and mortal tears, dear heart,
What pleasure can an old man's tears return?

My soul has almost reached the other side
And makes a shield against your kindly dart.
Charred wood will never make a new fire burn.

LI(ii)

Now give me back that time that held my passion,
Fervent and sweet, upon a gentle rein.
Give back the water and the fire again
If you desire my tears, my consummation.

Return those easy journeys which are now
So difficult to one of many years;
Give back that peaceful and angelic brow
Which snatched from nature all her secret powers.

Love, I am slow now to pursue your wings.
The nest is changed; it is, if I am right,
A blessed place where good intentions live.

Bring to the bow your arrows strong and bright,
And if death is no longer deaf to grief,
I'll find my peace among more blessed things.

LII

I do not need to look on outward forms
Of beauty which must die. I gaze within
Using your sight, finding a peace which calms.
Bringing such love, you banish every sin.

Even if she whom God created is
Not perfect outwardly, I ask no more,
For even if her loveliness has flaws,
She far transcends what I have seen before.

That man who is consumed by what must die
Can never quench his passion. Though it seems
To last for ever, it is transitory.

From sense not love, unruly passions come
And kill the soul. Our feeling's sanctified
Even here on earth, but more still when we have died.

LIII

An ardent love of a great beauty is
Not always wrong, for such a love can melt
The heart and let divine desire be felt;
The heavenly dart may penetrate with ease.

Love wakes prepared and soon adjusts its wings;
Such flight as it will make cannot compare
With those first stumbling steps, but these will bear
The soul up to the maker of all things.

To this, the love of which I speak aspires.
Woman is different and seldom worth
The fiery love which only strong hearts know.

One pulls me to the heavens, the other to earth.
One in the soul dwells, one in sensual fires
And to attain base things will draw the bow.

LIV

I see in your fair face, my dearest Lord,
That which in life I cannot fitly tell.
Your soul already, though flesh holds it still,
Has many times ascended to its God.

And if the vulgar and malignant crowd
Misunderstand the love with which we're blest,
Its worth is not affected in the least:
Our faith and honest love can still feel proud.

Earth is the meagre source of all that we
Can know while still fleshbound. To those who see
In the right way, it gives most copiously.

All that we have of wisdom and of faith
Derives from earth, and if I love you with
Fervour, I shall reach God and find sweet death.

LV

My Lord, you know that I know that you know
That I have come to be more close, more near.
You know that I know what is known to you,
Why then do we delay in greeting here?

If all that you have said is really true,
And if, which you admit, my trust is real,
Then break the wall dividing us, and know
A double strength can greater woes conceal.

If in you, I love only, my dear Lord,
What you love more yourself, do not be hurt
That with one soul another should accord.

That in your noble face which I love most
Is scarcely known by human mind and heart.
He who would see it must become a ghost.

LVI(i)

When you came back into this earthly prison,
It was as if an angel had sprung forth;
You were so full of that divine compassion
Which heals the mind and dignifies the earth.

This only draws me and with this alone
I fall in love, not with the outward grace
Of gentle features. Love will not grow less
When such a lasting good it fixes on.

In this way value always is detected
In proud and natural things. Heaven will not fail
To give what's needful when their birth takes place.

God in no other way has shown His grace
Than in a lovely and mortal veil
In which I find He is Himself reflected.

LVI(ii)

I know not whence it came and yet it surely
Sprang from that deathless soul which in your breast
Remains, yet seeks the universe entirely,
Healing the mind, making the whole earth blest.

This alone draws me, and with this alone
I fall in love, not with the outward grace
Of gentle features. Love will not grow less
When such a lasting good it fixes on.

If such a form should find new beauties growing
Upon itself as part of its own life,
Then from the sheath I can detect the knife.

Only in this way is God truly showing
His love, for heaven indeed can rival nature,
Letting a chaste love frame a lovelier creature.

LVII(i)

It passes from the eyes into the heart
In a split second. Thus all beauties may
Find by this means an open and broad way,
And thus, for thousands, their desires start.

I am afraid of love like this, being so
Burdened with sin, committing so much wrong.
Nor, though I seek a thousand souls among,
Can I find one whose loving is not low.

Yet love still lives however much it errs;
The world is full of it and man still flies
To things which often are a trap and curse.

If graces do not climb to heaven, then
Noble desires may, for otherwise,
What grief and torment to be born a man!

LVII(ii)

It passes from the eyes into the heart
In a split second. Thus all beauties may
Find by this means a wide and generous way;
And so, for countless men, desires start.

Burdened by grief and gripped by jealousy,
I am afraid of such a powerful passion.
Nor, among countless faces, can I see
One which in this life gives me consolation.

If mortal beauty satisfies desire
Completely, then it did not come from heaven;
Such strong emotion comes from human fire.

But if I pass beyond this and have striven
For heavenly things, I need not be afraid
That I by base desires shall be waylaid.

LVIII

When to my inward eyes, both weak and strong,
The idol of my heart appears, I know
That always in between us death will go;
It frightens me as it drives me along.

Yet, strangely, such an outrage gives me hope
And I take courage from so rare a fate.
Indomitable love moves in great state
And thus he puts his strong defences up:

Dying, he says, can never happen twice,
Nor is one born again. If a man dies
By fire when he already is aflame

With burning love, then death can do no harm.
Such love's the magnet of all burning hearts
Which, purged, returns to God from where it starts.

LIX

Only through fire can the smith pull and stretch
Metal into the shape of his design.
Only through fire can the artist reach
Pure gold which only furnaces refine.

Nor can the phoenix rare itself remake
Unless it first be burnt. For my part, I
Hope to ascend triumphantly on high
Where death fulfills, where time itself must break.

The fire of which I speak has brought salvation,
I find in it new powers and restoration
Although I seemed already with the dead.

Since by fire nature reaches up to heaven
I may, through it, be reconciled, forgiven,
For it must surely bear me overhead.

LX(i)

Sometimes hope rises strongly with desire,
And surely such a hope may not be held
As false; if heaven is angry with such fire,
Then to what end did God create the world?

What better reason can there be to love,
Than to give glory to the God on high?
He who is pleased with you dwells up above,
And every good heart he will purify.

Only false hopes can claim a love that dies.
Such love depends on beauty which grows less,
And the swift change of mortal loveliness.

Sweet is that hope which in the modest heart
Is steadfast though all surface things depart!
Such faithful love's a pledge of paradise.

13. STUDY FOR THE CASCINA CARTOON

14. CHRIST ON THE CROSS

15. STUDIES FOR THE *Descent from the Cross*

16. RESURRECTION

LX(ii)

At times, pure love may justly be equated
With fervent hope; nor need it be deceived.
If by all human loves the heavens are grieved,
Then to what end was the whole world created?

If I indeed honour and love you, Lord,
And if I burn, it is a heavenly calm
That emanates from you and makes me warm;
Such peace is far removed from all discord.

True love is not a passion which can die,
Or which depends on beauty that must fade;
Nor is it subject to a changing face.

That love is true and holy which finds place
Within a modest heart, and which is made,
Far above earth, a pledge of love on high.

LXI

ON THE DEATH OF VITTORIA COLONNA

If my rough hammer makes a human form
And carves it in the hard, unyielding stone,
My hand is guided, does not move alone,
But follows where that other worker came.

Yet the first worker, God, remains above,
Whose very motion makes all loveliness.
To make a tool I need a tool, but his
Power is the first cause and makes all things move.

That stroke which in the forge is raised most high
Has the most strength. Now she who lifted me,
Has, by her death, been raised much higher still.

So I am left unfinished now until
She gives her help to God himself that I
May be completed, not abandoned lie.

LXII

ON THE DEATH OF THE SAME

When she who was the cause of all my sighs
Withdrew both from the world and from my eyes,
Nature itself was full of shame to see
Men weeping at the loss of such as she.

But nature may not boast as once it did.
Not it but death has quenched this sun of suns.
But death by love is conquered; love has laid
This glorious creature with the blessed ones.

Thus death, so pitiless, is now deceived;
It has no power to harm such pure perfection,
Or dim her triumph, as it once believed.

History is shining with her soul's reflection
Since she, though dead, lives more abundantly,
She, who would never leave us willingly.

LXIII

Ah yes, when I was fortunate and when
Phoebus blazed down on every hill for me,
I should have risen from the crude earth then,
Using his wings to seek death willingly.

Those promises were vain; it is too late,
For now my soul, ungrateful, full of guilt,
Lacking both wisdom and what once it felt,
Is now exiled, for Heaven has shut the gate.

I climbed the hills; feathers were wings to me,
Phoebus himself lifted my feet, and I
Thought death itself was wonderful indeed.

I die now without wings and cannot be
Borne up to Heaven. Even my memories die.
Afflicted thus, what comfort can I plead?

LXIV

ON THE DEATH OF THE SAME

What wonder is it if, when near the fire,
I burned and melted, now that it is cold
I am consumed still with a fierce desire
And turn to ashes, sad and unfulfilled.

I saw the place, so burning and so bright,
Where my great torment hung. It only could
Turn death into a gay fiesta mood,
And make me happy at the mere sight.

But since the splendour of that fire, which would
So nourish me, is snatched into the dark
By Heaven, I am a lighted coal concealed:

And if by words of love I can't be healed,
Then I am nothing now, not even a spark,
But turn to ashes what the fire once held.

LXV

Already now my life has run its course,
And, like a fragile boat on a rough sea,
I reach the place which everyone must cross
And give account of life's activity.

Now I know well it was a fantasy
That made me think art could be made into
An idol or a king. Though all men do
This, they do it half-unwillingly.

The loving thoughts, so happy and so vain,
Are finished now. A double death comes near—
The one is sure, the other is a threat.

Painting and sculpture cannot any more
Quieten the soul that turns to God again
To God who, on the cross, for us was set.

LXVI

By the world's vanities I've been distracted,
And thus have squandered hours which should have been
Reserved for God. His mercy I've rejected,
And my misuse of it has made me sin.

The knowledge which makes others wise has made
Me blind. I recognise my faults too late.
Hope lessens, yet, before desires fade,
Of friend, dissolve my self-love and self-hate.

And God, divide, I beg, the road that leads
To Heaven; I cannot climb its length alone,
I need your help through all the snares and strife.

Help me to loathe the world and all its deeds;
I'll cast its beauties out but to atone,
And find the promise of eternal life.

LXVII

There is no lower thing on earth than I
Conceive myself to be when I lack you.
My weak and tired spirit makes me sigh
For pardon for all things I've failed to do.

Stretch down to me, Oh God, that powerful chain
That knots all heavenly gifts. Such faith and trust
Are what I long forever to attain;
It is my fault I am not fully blest.

The more I think of faith, more rare and good
It seems, and even greater may it be
Since all the world depends on it for peace.

You never were a miser of your blood:
If Heaven is locked to every other key,
What kind of gifts of mercy, then, are these?

LXVIII

By cross and grace and every kind of pain,
I am convinced, sir, we shall meet in Heaven.
Yet, long before such joy, we can attain,
It seems to me, the good things earth has given.

If sharp and bitter ways through hills and sea
Part me from you, my zeal has set at naught
Such icy obstacles. And, inwardly,
Nothing can slow or stop the wings of thought.

In my own thoughts I am with you for ever.
I weep and talk and nothing now can sever
Me from my dead Urbino who, were he

Alive, might now indeed converse with me.
But he is dead, so by another way
I hope to lodge with him without delay.

LXIX

My death is certain but the hour unsure,
Life is so brief and little now have I;
So sweet it is to sense, yet cannot lure
The soul. My spirit prays that I may die.

The world is bad, and evil customs still
Defeat good habits, cast good actions out.
The light's extinguished, pride and daring will
Make false things triumph, call the truth in doubt.

Oh God, when will that time arrive which he,
Who trusts in you, expects? Hope falls away,
And fatal to the soul is great delay.

What good is it that light and clarity
Should shine for others if, before it dies,
The soul is lost in such uncertainties?

LXX

Loaded with years and full of all my sins,
Rooted in habits evil and yet strong,
I feel two deaths approach me. Now begins
The heart's division, poisoned for so long.

Nor have I all the forces which I need
To change my life and love, custom and fate.
Only your grace and power can intercede
And guide our steps before it is too late.

It is not now enough, Oh Lord, that I
Wish to be made anew. I cannot be
The same as when, from nothing, you made me.

I beg you—halve that way so steep and high
Before you take my body from my soul:
And may I come back purified and whole.

LXXI

Now that I need men's pity and compassion,
And can no longer scoff and laugh at all
The faults of others, now my soul must fall
Unguided, lacking its own domination.

Only one flag can I now serve beneath,
And with it conquer life. I speak of faith.
Only with this can I face the attack
Of all my foes, when other help I lack.

Oh flesh, Oh blood, Oh wood, Oh pain extreme!
Let all my sins be purified through you
From whom I came, as did my father too.

So good you are, your pity is supreme;
Only your help can save my evil fate:
So close to death, so far from God my state.

LXXII

Then let me see you everywhere I go.
If merely mortal beauty makes me burn,
How much more strongly I shall shine and glow
When to your fiery love at last I turn.

Dear God, I call and plead with you alone,
For only you can help my blinding pain;
You only have the power to sustain
My courage. I am helpless on my own.

This everlasting spirit, which you gave
To me on earth, is locked within a frail
Body and doomed to an unhappy fate.

What can I do? Myself I cannot save;
Without your strength I certainly shall fail.
Only divine power can improve my state.

LXXIII

Unburdened by the body's fierce demands,
And now at last released from my frail boat,
Dear God, I put myself into your hands;
Smooth the rough waves on which my ship must float.

The thorns, the nails, the wounds in both your palms,
The gentleness, the pity on your face—
For great repentance, these have promised grace.
My soul will find salvation in your arms.

And let not justice only fill your eyes,
But mercy too. Oh temper your severe
Judgment with tenderness, relieve my burden.

Let your own blood remove my faults and clear
My guilt, and let your grace so strongly rise
That I am granted an entire pardon.

LXXIV(i)

Simply the longing for more years to live
Seems to hold out a promise. Yet I know
That death's approach is never made more slow,
That only sorrows have the power to give

A sense of halting. Yet how foolish is
A longing for more life and pleasure when
God is found best in human miseries.
The happier life, the more it hurts again.

And if, dear God, your grace assails my heart
And sets it burning with a fiery zeal,
Which deep within my spirit I can feel,

Then I from my own gifts would gladly part
And rise to Heaven at once, since I am sure
My good desires on earth will not endure.

LXXIV(ii)

Often, I think, a great desire may
Hold out the promise of more time to me.
Yet death has power to whittle me away
The more I live and breathe delightedly.

What better time for my sure transformation
Than when I pray, in grief, to God above?
Then lead me, Lord, to my true destination,
And all my earthly cares and joys remove.

For in this way your grace assails my heart
With faith and all its strong and fervent zeal.
From such a comfort I would never part.

Alone, I shall for certain always fail:
Then plant in me that faith such as you give
To angels who, without you, cannot live.

LXXV

I wish, God, for some end I do not will.
Between the fire and heart a veil of ice
Puts out the fire. My pen will not move well,
So that the sheet on which I'm working lies.

I pay you mere lip-service, then I grieve;
Love does not reach my heart, I do not know
How to admit that grace which would relieve
My state and crush the arrogance I show.

Oh tear away that veil, God, break that wall
Which with its strength refuses to let in
The sun whose light has vanished from the world.

Send down the promised light to bless and hold
Your lovely bride. So may I seek for all
I need in you, both end there and begin.

LXXVI

Those souls for whom you died were sad as well
As happy that you chose death for their sake.
The blood you shed had locked the doors of Hell,
And opened Heaven for all mankind to take.

Happy they were because you had redeemed
Man from his first mistake and final loss.
But they were sad such suffering had claimed
Your flesh which died for all men on the cross.

Heaven gave a sign that she had seen it all;
Her eyes grew dim, the earth beneath her showed
A gulf, the waters rushed, the mountains shook.

Christ snatched the Fathers from their dark abode
But sent the devils to a greater fall;
All baptised men for his own joy he took.

LXXVII

Although it saddens me and causes pain,
The past, which is not with me any more,
Brings me relief, since all that I abhor—
My sin and guilt—will not come back again.

Precious it is to me because I learn,
Before death comes, how brief is happiness
But sad also, since when at last I turn
For pardon, grace may yet refuse to bless.

Although, Oh God, your promise I attend,
It is too much to ask you to forgive
Those who for pardon have so long delayed.

But in the blood you shed, I understand
What recompense and mercy you've displayed,
Showering your precious gifts that we may live.

LXXVIII

Dear to me is sleep: still more, being made of stone.
While pain and guilt still linger here below,
Blindness and numbness—these please me alone;
Then do not wake me, keep your voices low.

INDEX OF FIRST LINES

K52